Closing Time

by Owen McCafferty

NT
TRANS
FORM
AT!ON

TRANSFORMATION

29 April–21 September 2002

The Lyttelton *Transformation* project is vital to my idea of the
National Theatre because it both celebrates and challenges our
identity. What do we want the National to be? We must draw on
our heritage, on our recent past, and on the talent of the next
generation. I want a thriving new audience, including a body
of young people under 30 with a theatre-going habit, a new
generation of artistic and administrative talent committed to
taking the National forward and a realization of the varied
potential within this glorious building.

Trevor Nunn Director of the National Theatre

Transformation is thirteen world premieres, hosted in two new
theatre spaces, with special low ticket prices. The National's most
traditional auditorium, the Lyttelton, has been transformed by
a sweep of seats from circle to stage to create a new intimacy
between actor and audience. At the same time the Loft has been
created – a fully flexible 100-seat theatre. *Transformation* will
introduce new generations of theatre makers and theatre
audiences to one of the most exciting theatres in the world.

Mick Gordon Artistic Associate
Joseph Smith Associate Producer

Transformation has received major creative input from the Studio –
the National Theatre's laboratory for new work and its engine
room for new writing – and celebrates the Studio's continuing
investment in theatre makers.

Closing Time

by Owen McCafferty

In order of speaking

Vera	PAM FERRIS
Iggy	PATRICK O'KANE
Robbie	JIM NORTON
Joe	LALOR RODDY
Alec	KIERAN AHERN

Director	JAMES KERR
Designer	RAE SMITH
Lighting Designer	STEVE BARNETT
Sound Designer	RICH WALSH
Company Voice Work	PATSY RODENBURG & KATE GODFREY

Assistant Director	Kirstie Jones
Production Manager	Katrina Gilroy
Stage Manager	Stuart Calder
Deputy Stage Manager	Lotte Buchan
Assistant Stage Manager	Marion Marrs
Costume Supervisor	Sharon Robinson
Casting	Maggie Lunn

OPENING: Loft 9 September 2002

Copies of this cast list in braille or large print are available at the Information Desk

KIERAN AHERN
ALEC

Kieran Ahern's **theatre** credits include Sebastian Barry's *Hinterland* (Out of Joint/National) and Smith in the original cast of *The Steward of Christendom* (Out of Joint/Royal Court) directed by Max Stafford Clark, which played in London, Dublin, Luxembourg, Sydney, Wellington and New York; and Jim in *The Weir* (Royal Court) directed by Ian Rickson. The production toured extensively to London, Dublin, Brussels, Toronto and Broadway. Other recent credits include the Druid/Royal Court production of Marina Carr's *On Raftery's Hill* (touring to Galway, Dublin, London and Washington; *The Overcoat* (Dublin Theatre Festival); *Tartuffe* (Gate Theatre); *Normal* (Meridian); *The Illusion* (Charabanc) and *Lady Windermere's Fan* (Rough Magic). **Film** and **TV** credits include *The Last September*, *Titanic Town*, *The Matchmaker*, *Meteor*, *Love and Rage*, *Before I Sleep*, *Inspector Morse*, *Amongst Women*, *The Governor*, *Amazing Love Stories*, *Edward No Hands*, *The Widow's Son* and *White*.

PAM FERRIS
VERA

Pam Ferris' **theatre** credits include 50 plays in New Zealand before coming to the UK in 1972. She spent 5 years working with Mike Alfreds for Shared Experience; appeared in many plays at the Royal Court and for Out of Joint; *Roots* at the NT; and recently *The Vagina Monologues* in the West End. Extensive **TV** includes playing Ma Larkin in *The Darling Buds of May*, and 4 years in *Where The Heart Is*. Most recently: *Sweet Revenge*, *Doc Martin*, *Linda Green*, *Pollyanna*, and *Paradise Heights*. **Film** includes Roald Dahl's *Matilda*, directed by Danny De Vito, with whom she worked again in 2001 on *Death to Smoochy*.

JIM NORTON
ROBBIE

Theatre credits include *A Chorus of Disapproval*, *St Joan*, *Way Upstream*, *Hamlet*, *Tamburlaine*, *Emigrés*, *Comedians*, *Bedroom Farce* and *Playboy of the Western World* (National); *The Weir* (London and Broadway); *The Contractor* and *The Changing Room* (Royal Court); *Red Roses for Me*, *Boss Grady's Boys*, *White Woman Street* and *She Stoops to Folly* (Abbey Theatre, Dublin); *Port Authority* (Ambassadors & Gate Dublin); *Come On Over* (Gate Dublin); and *Juno and the Paycock* (Roundabout NY). **Film** credits include *Straw Dogs*, *Hidden Agenda*, *Memoirs of an Invisible Man*, *Conspiracy of Silence*, *Harry Potter and the Chamber of Secrets*.

PATRICK O'KANE
IGGY

Patrick O'Kane's **theatre** credits include *Playboy of the Western World*, *Peer Gynt* and *Romeo and Juliet* (National); *Medea* and *The House* (Abbey Theatre); *Miss Julie* and *Donny Boy* (Royal Exchange); *Sweet Bird of Youth* and *Edward II* (Citizens); *Macbeth* (West Yorkshire Playhouse); and *The Grapes of Wrath* (The Crucible). **TV** includes *As the Beast Sleeps*, *Any Time Now*, *A Rap at the Door* and *In Deep*. **Film** includes *The Wayfarer*, *Perdie*, *Octane* and *When the Sky Falls*.

LALOR RODDY
JOE

Theatre credits include *The Tempest*, *Macbeth*, *Observe the Sons of Ulster*, *Barbaric Comedies* and *A Little World of Our Own* (Abbey Theatre, Dublin); *King Baby*, *Amphibians*, *Shadows* and *Measure for Measure* (RSC); *Death and The Maiden*, *Volunteers*, *A Doll's House* and *Pentecost* (Tinderbox & Prime Cut). **Film** and **TV** credits include *Love & Rage*, *Making the Cut*, *The Double*, *'81*, *Arise and Go Now* and *Rules of Engagement*. He was a founder member of Tinderbox.

OWEN McCAFFERTY

AUTHOR

Born in 1961, Owen McCafferty lives in Belfast. He was writer on attachment to the National Theatre Studio in 1999. His most recent work includes No Place like Home, Mojo Mickybo and Shoot the Crow. His plays for radio include The Elasticity of Supply and Demand and The Law of Diminishing Returns.

JAMES KERR

DIRECTOR

James Kerr studied Classics at University College, London, and trained at LAMDA. He was awarded the Quercus Trust Bursary, and worked at the National Theatre Studio as Director on Attachment. Since then his **directing** credits include Twelfth Night (Liverpool Playhouse); Aeschylus' Suppliants (Gate Theatre); Katherine Burger's Morphic Resonance (Donmar Warehouse); Rita Dove's The Darker Face of the Earth (National); George Farquhar's The Recruiting Officer (Chichester Festival Theatre) and David Harrower's Presence (Royal Court Theatre Upstairs).

RAE SMITH

DESIGNER

Previous work for the National includes The Visit and The Street of Crocodiles. Recent work includes Magic Flute (Scottish Opera), Port and A Midsummer Night's Dream (Royal Exchange Manchester), The Prince of Homburg (RSC/Lyric Hammersmith) and Johnson Over Jordan (West Yorkshire Playhouse). Other credits include Juno and the Paycock (Donmar/Roundabout NY), The Weir (Royal Court/West End/Broadway), Endgame (Donmar), and The Servant (Lyric Hammersmith). www.rae-smith.co.uk.

STEVE BARNETT

LIGHTING DESIGNER

Lighting credits include The Mentalists, The Shadow of a Boy, Sing Yer Heart Out for the Lads, Sparkleshark (National), Carmen and L'Elisir d'Amore (Surrey Opera), Bedroom Farce and Blithe Spirit (Redgrave Theatre), Sympathetic Magic (Finborough), La Veneziana (Etcetera) and Evelyn Glennie's multi-media show Shadow touring UK and Europe. He has worked at many regional theatres and at the National since 1994. He relit Frogs (NT Education tour) and has been Assistant to the Lighting Designer on My Fair Lady, The Winter's Tale, The Waiting Room, Mother Courage and Peter Pan, relighting the revival.

RICH WALSH

SOUND DESIGNER

Previous sound designs include: The Associate, Sanctuary, The Mentalists, The Shadow of a Boy, Free, Sing Yer Heart Out for the Lads, The Walls (National); Exposure, Under The Blue Sky, On Raftery's Hill, Sacred Heart, Trust, Choice (Royal Court); Julie Burchill is Away (Soho Theatre); 50 Revolutions (Whitehall); The Boy Who Left Home, The Nation's Favourite (UK tours); Yllana's 666 (Riverside Studios); Strike Gently Away From Body, Blavatsky (Young Vic Studio); Body And Soul, Soap Opera, The Baltimore Waltz (Upstairs At The Gatehouse); Small Craft Warnings (Pleasance); The Taming of the Shrew, Macbeth (Japanese tour); Dirk, Red Noses (Oxford Playhouse); The Wizard of Oz, The Winter's Tale (Old Fire Station, Oxford).

KIRSTIE JONES

ASSISTANT DIRECTOR

Kirstie Jones graduated from Manchester University with a degree in drama. She specialized in teaching drama to prisoners and has worked in a number of institutions. She went on to produce and perform in several plays in Manchester and at the Edinburgh Fringe and has also written for the stage. She trained at LAMDA and has recently directed a showcase of new writing for the Academy.

The Loft Theatre was created with the help of the Royal National Theatre Foundation.

The *Transformation* season is supported by Edward and Elissa Annunziato, Peter Wolff Theatre Trust, and by a gift from the estate of André Deutsch.

Many of the projects in the *Transformation* season were developed in the National Theatre Studio.

ON WORD graphics designed by typographer Alan Kitching using original wood letters.

The National's workshops are responsible for, on these productions: Armoury; Costume; Props & furniture; Scenic construction; Scenic painting; Wigs

TRANSFORMATION SEASON TEAM (Loft)
ARTISTIC ASSOCIATE Mick Gordon
ASSOCIATE PRODUCER Joseph Smith
ADMINISTRATOR Sarah Nicholson
LOFT THEATRE DESIGNER Will Bowen
FRONT OF HOUSE DESIGNER Jo Maund
FRONT OF HOUSE DESIGN PRODUCTION MANAGER Gavin Gibson
LITERARY MANAGER Jack Bradley
PLANNING PROJECT MANAGER Paul Jozefowski
RESIDENT DIRECTOR – LOFT Paul Miller
PRODUCTION CO-ORDINATOR Katrina Gilroy
PRODUCTION MANAGER – LOFT REALISATION Jo Maund
PRODUCTION ASSISTANTS – LOFT REALISATION Alan Bain and Gavin Gibson
LOFT LIGHTING REALISATION & TECHNICIANS Mike Atkinson, Steve Barnett,
    Pete Bull, Huw Llewellyn, Cat Silver
LOFT SOUND REALISATION Adam Rudd, Rich Walsh
LOFT STAGE TECHNICIANS Danny O'Neill, Stuart Smith
MODEL MAKERS Aaron Marsden, Riette Hayes-Davies
GRAPHIC DESIGNERS Stephen Cummiskey, Patrick Eley
PROGRAMME EDITOR Dinah Wood
PRESS Lucinda Morrison, Mary Parker, Gemma Gibb
MARKETING David Hamilton-Peters
PRODUCTION PHOTOGRAPHER Sheila Burnett
THEATRE MANAGER John Langley

Thanks to the following people who were part of the original Lyttelton Development Group: Ushi Bagga, Alice Dunne, Annie Eves-Boland, Jonathan Holloway, Gareth James, Mark Jonathan, Holly Kendrick, Paul Jozefowski, Angus MacKechnie, Tim Redfern, Chris Shutt, Matt Strevens, Jane Suffling, Nicola Wilson, Dinah Wood, Lucy Woollatt

NATIONAL THEATRE BOOKSHOP
The National's Bookshop in the Main Entrance foyer on the ground floor stocks a wide range of theatre-related books. Texts of all the plays in the Loft during the Transformation season, and of the plays in *Channels (France)* are available from the NT Bookshop at £2. T: 020 7452 3456; www.nationaltheatre.org.uk/bookshop

TRANSFORMATION SEASON

IN THE LYTTELTON

A co-production between the National Theatre & Théâtre National de Chaillot

The PowerBook . . . . 9 May–4 June
from a novel by Jeanette Winterson
devised by Jeanette Winterson, Deborah Warner & Fiona Shaw
Director Deborah Warner

A Prayer for Owen Meany . . . . 10–29 June
a novel by John Irving
adapted by Simon Bent
Director Mick Gordon

A collaboration between the National Theatre & Trestle Theatre Company

The Adventures of the Stoneheads . . . . 4–13 July
written & directed by Toby Wilsher

A collaboration between the National Theatre & Mamaloucos Circus

The Birds . . . . 23 July–14 August
by Aristophanes, in a new verse version by Sean O'Brien
Director Kathryn Hunter

Play Without Words . . . . 20 August–14 September
devised & directed by Matthew Bourne

IN THE LOFT

Sing Yer Heart Out for the Lads . . . . 29 April–15 May
by Roy Williams
Director Simon Usher

Free . . . . 20 May–8 June
by Simon Bowen
Director Thea Sharrock

Life After Life . . . . 28 May–8 June
a reportage play by Paul Jepson & Tony Parker
Director Paul Jepson

The Shadow of a Boy . . . . 13–29 June
by Gary Owen
Director Erica Whyman

The Mentalists . . . . 4–20 July
by Richard Bean
Director Sean Holmes

Sanctuary . . . . 25 July–10 August
by Tanika Gupta
Director Hettie Macdonald

The Associate . . . . 15–31 August
by Simon Bent
Director Paul Miller

Closing Time . . . . 4–21 September
by Owen McCafferty
Director James Kerr

NATIONAL THEATRE STUDIO &
TRANSFORMATION

All the plays in the LOFT are co-produced with the National Theatre Studio. The Studio is the National's laboratory for research and development, providing a workspace outside the confines of the rehearsal room and stage, where artists can experiment and develop their skills.

As part of its training for artists there is an on-going programme of classes, workshops, seminars, courses and masterclasses. Residencies have also been held in Edinburgh, Vilnius, Belfast and South Africa, enabling artists from a wider community to share and exchange experiences.

Central to the Studio's work is a commitment to new writing. The development and support of writers is demonstrated through play readings, workshops, short-term attachments, bursaries and sessions with senior writers. Work developed there continually reaches audiences throughout the country and overseas, on radio, film and television as well as at the National and other theatres. Most recent work includes the award-winning plays *Further than the Furthest Thing* by Zinnie Harris (Tron Theatre, Glasgow; Traverse, Edinburgh, and NT), *The Waiting Room* by Tanika Gupta (NT) and *Gagarin Way* by Gregory Burke (in association with Traverse, Edinburgh; NT; and at the Arts Theatre), *The Walls* by Colin Teevan (NT), *Accomplices* by Simon Bent, *Mr England* by Richard Bean (in association with Sheffield Theatres) and *The Slight Witch* by Paul Lucas (in association with Birmingham Rep), as well as a season of five new plays from around the world with the Gate Theatre, and *Missing Reel* by Toby Jones at the Traverse during the Edinburgh Festival 2001. *Gagarin Way* and *Further than the Furthest Thing* were part of SPRINGBOARDS – a series of partnerships created by the Royal National Theatre Studio with other theatres, enabling work by emerging writers to reach a wider audience.

Direct Action, a collaboration between The Studio and the Young Vic, is an initiative that provides young directors with an opportunity to work on the main stage of the Young Vic. Two plays were co-produced in the autumn of 2001: Max Frisch's *Andorra*, directed by Gregory Thompson; and David Rudkin's *Afore Night Come*, directed by Rufus Norris, who won the Evening Standard award for Best Newcomer for this production.

For the Royal National Theatre Studio

HEAD OF STUDIO	Sue Higginson
STUDIO MANAGER	Matt Strevens
TECHNICAL MANAGER	Eddie Keogh
INTERNATIONAL PROJECTS MANAGER	Philippe Le Moine

NT

Royal National Theatre
South Bank, London SE1 9PX
Box Office: 020 7452 3000
Information: 020 7452 3400

Registered Charity No: 224223

The chief aims of the National, under the direction of Trevor Nunn, are to present a diverse repertoire, embracing classic, new and neglected plays; to present these plays to the very highest standards; and to give audiences a wide choice.

All kinds of other events and services are on offer – short early-evening Platform performances; work for children and education work; free live entertainment both inside and outdoors at holiday times; exhibitions; live foyer music; backstage tours; bookshops; plenty of places to eat and drink; and easy car-parking. The nearby Studio acts as a resource for research and development for actors, writers and directors.

We send productions on tour, both in this country and abroad, and do all we can, through ticket-pricing, to make the NT accessible to everyone.

The National's home on the South Bank, opened in 1976, contains three separate theatres: the Olivier, the Lyttelton, and the Cottesloe and – during *Transformation* – a fourth: the Loft. It is open to the public all day, six days a week, fifty-two weeks a year. Stage by Stage – an exhibition on the NT's history, can be seen in the Olivier Gallery.

A Nick Hern Book

Closing Time first published in Great Britain in 2002
as a paperback original by Nick Hern Books Limited,
14 Larden Road, London W3 7ST, in association
with the National Theatre, London

Typeset by Country Setting, Kingsdown, Kent CT14 8ES
Printed in Great Britain by Bookmarque, Croydon, Surrey

ISBN 1 85459 691 8

A CIP catalogue record for this book is available from
the British Library

CLOSING TIME

Owen McCafferty

For my mother
Rosemary
1936–2002

Characters

ROBBIE, *early sixties*

VERA, *late fifties*

JOE, *early sixties*

IGGY, *mid thirties*

ALEC, *early fifties*

Setting

*A grubby pub/hotel. All the action takes place in the pub.
There are two exits, one to the hotel the other to the street.
At one end of the bar there is a large television screen.
The television is always on but the sound is never turned up.
At the other end of the bar is a public pay phone. When people
are not directly involved in conversation they watch the
television, except Joe who sits with his back to the screen.*

Note: if / is a moment then – is half a moment

*This text went to press before the end of rehearsals, so may
differ from the play as performed.*

*Morning. The bar is locked up. Joe is asleep at the counter, an
empty bottle of vodka in front of him. Robbie is slumped over
a table, surrounded by empty Babycham bottles. Robbie wakes
and surveys his surroundings. He hears Vera and Iggy coming
down the stairs and pretends to be asleep. Vera unlocks the
hotel door then enters, followed by Iggy, who is badly hungover.
Once in the bar Vera unlocks the door leading to the street.*

VERA   smell this dump / same bloody stink every day –
fills the air it does / ya think other people live like
this / bet ya the don't

IGGY   *sits at counter beside pay phone* / get us a pint vera
will ye – am dyin / fuckin head's rippin open /
bustin

VERA   the shutter'll only wake 'im – a don't want that yet –
if yer that bad am sure there's somethin on the table

IGGY   that's not drink

VERA   ya take enough a it it is / should eat somethin /
want me t'make somethin t'eat / a've t'do breakfast
for joe anyway

IGGY   *without waking Robbie he takes a bottle of
Babycham* / kiddin me / food / no eats for three
days / grub be bad news right now / eat in a coupla
days time maybe / need a gargle – best thing

VERA   the world be in a panic without it – aye

IGGY   a've knocked it on the head a few times / at the
moment that wouldn't be right though

VERA   *stands on a chair to open the window beside the
front door* / let some air in here / first thing in the
mornin's bad / end up like mickey an donald there

IGGY   will a fuck / know what am at / there's a cut off
line or whatever / it's in yer head – it tells ye /

that's the time t'pay attention t'what yer bein told /
up t'that point ya wang away without – whatever –
don't know – fucked

VERA   many's a man's sat here an said that iggy

IGGY   am the first t'mean it though – there's a difference /
know what am at

VERA   all know what we're at

IGGY   vera what's the score with readies here / am skint –
don't want t'be startin the day off with nothin / any
chance ya could – y'know / give it back t'ye
whenever am sorted out – it's just – y'know

VERA   a've a few quid / keep ya goin

IGGY   some women vera / not many like ye

VERA   *sits beside him and gives him some money from her
bag* / too good for this kip

IGGY   darlin ya are / *drinks* / ya not openin up

VERA   in a minute

IGGY   cat rough / when my da was on the piss – first pop
every mornin boke his ring / couldn't handle it /
shouldn't a took it then / we should all do what he
did / pack yer bags an sling yer hook

VERA   do a look as if a haven't thought about it / there's
mornin's a wake up an think a can't take any more
a this / somethin eatin away at me / a don't know
what it is – but it's in this place / come down the
stairs he's lyin there / must be another way – keep
thinkin that

IGGY   know what ya mean / i go for days not knowin
what the fuck's goin on aroun me sometimes /
always thinkin if a were somewhere else a'd know
what the fuck was goin on / always somewhere
else like innit

VERA   my case has been packed more than once / i've one
lyin in the back a the wardrobe from years back –

packed an all / nothin in it bloody fit me now / but sure what would he do / he'd be in the gutter – left on his own / couldn't leave 'im – couldn't bring 'im with ya

IGGY   fuck 'im / let 'im paddle his own dixie / it's the makin a people bein left on their jacks / only get one crack at it vera – do what ya should be doin / none a that regret chat – fuck that

VERA   finish yer drink an we'll go back up stairs / the day's work can wait / don't worry about him – his head'll not raise until that shutter rattles

IGGY   vera / ya must be jokin / look at the state a me – fit for fuck all am / couldn't climb the stairs never mind givin it that other trick / besides that – he might – y'know / sortin out that situation – jesus

VERA   you sure?

IGGY   better believe it am sure

VERA   don't be comin lookin me t'night

IGGY   yer the one does the lookin

VERA   a wont be again

IGGY   give me a break will ye / vera – just let me get through the fuckin pint will ye / the state am in at the moment – this is the crack a dawn y'know / lets get settled here / we'll see what happens later / let me – my head needs straightened out a bit that's all

VERA   get yerself straightened out – that's the most important thing

Iggy watches television. Vera lights a cigarette.

IGGY   good big box

VERA   one a pisspot's brainwaves / thought it would bring the punters back in

IGGY   where's the chat t'turn the soun up?

VERA   he threw it out

IGGY   threw it out why?

VERA   ask 'im – a don't know

IGGY   politics or talks or somethin t'day

VERA   gab all the want – not be buyin lunch here

IGGY   suits / men in suits / wives must all be blind lettin 'em go out like that

VERA   i look like a care?

IGGY   some fuckin talkin done – wha

VERA   dummies meetin in the house

IGGY   aye / my da used t'say there's too much fuckin talk in the world / take the spondolix off 'em – no fuckin about then

VERA   *puts cigarette out* / get somethin done here

IGGY   aye vera open up

Vera takes keys from her handbag and opens the shutters. Robbie wakes. Iggy puts his empty bottle of Babycham in the bin beside him. Joe stirs but doesn't fully wake. Vera wipes the counter down and puts a glass of vodka in front of Joe. She pays for the drink with coins on the counter. Vera pulls Iggy a pint. After exchanging glances with Vera he pays for the pint. Vera moves to Robbie and starts to clear the bottles around him.

VERA   a think we're out a babycham

ROBBIE are we / hardly be missed / not that popular am told

VERA   popular enough with those who have t'break in t'the yard t'get it

ROBBIE anythin be popular with those people

VERA   what type a man drinks a crate a babycham

ROBBIE a thirsty one

VERA   no man at all

ROBBIE   very good / thank you vera / it wasn't the
           babycham dampened that flame dear

VERA   pisspot

ROBBIE   aye

IGGY   robbie why's there no chat for the soun on the box?

ROBBIE   still here are ye

IGGY   why's there no chat?

ROBBIE   cause i own this place an a don't want there t'be
           any chat that's why

IGGY   grumpy head on

ROBBIE   watch it an keep quiet

           Vera sits facing Robbie.

VERA   my love

ROBBIE   yes dear

VERA   all set for t'day / head clear is it darling / sharp?

ROBBIE   razor blade – sweetness

VERA   yer the man t'handle things

ROBBIE   what is there t'handle / ask the guy for the readies
           – get the readies – sort it out

VERA   am not goin with ya

ROBBIE   that meant t'make a difference is it / i've organised
           it – i'll handle it / no problem t'me / better off on
           me own / man t'man – few gargles – that's the way
           t'do business / you don't go – be fine

VERA   let you out on yer own?

ROBBIE   a know that

VERA   be lost ya would / wee soul – wee lost soul / have
           ya the books sorted out yet / he'll want t'look at
           books

ROBBIE   it'll be done / figures has t'be fresh in my head

VERA	aye – fresh in yer head / do it right / am goin open up the kitchen an get joes breakfast sorted out / cause if i don't nobody will
ROBBIE	a wee cupa tea
VERA	it's what i live an die for robbie
ROBBIE	thank you
VERA	yer welcome / ya want some tea?
IGGY	stick with this – mixin them give ya the sickybad
VERA	this place stinks / yous all need a bloody good hosin / a take it yer not eatin
ROBBIE	maybe later
VERA	aye / the books
ROBBIE	aye

Vera exits to hotel. Robbie sits beside Iggy.

IGGY	robbie
ROBBIE	get yer head down alright last night – aye
IGGY	with the gargle in me – out like a light / ya know the score yerself
ROBBIE	room up at the top?
IGGY	at the top – aye / up at the top – oh aye
ROBBIE	vera sort ya out did she?
IGGY	sort me out?
ROBBIE	aye / blankets / freeze the cleavers off ye up there / bad for business if guests get the cleavers froze off 'em
IGGY	soun it was / blankets – everythin – soun
ROBBIE	a good woman she is / likes t'look after people / it's in her nature
IGGY	aye good woman / can't hear but a think united's sellin their keeper or somethin / face is up there must be sellin 'im / wanker anyway he is

ROBBIE   i'm a funny fucker – know that / could be a stretcher case an still remember everythin said t'me / last night talkin t'you – a remember that

IGGY   not worth rememberin / a lot a balls was it

ROBBIE   about how fucked up ya felt / which yer entitled t'do / wantin advice ya were / a told ye t'take yerself off home – best place for ye / ya seemed t'reckon that / yer still here?

IGGY   rocket fuel an that robbie – all the plans go out the fuckin winda / ya know yerself

ROBBIE   that right / ya hear what the lovely vera an me were talkin about there?

IGGY   a wouldn't do that – privacy an all that robbie – no way

ROBBIE   did ya hear?

IGGY   a wee bit at the end – no more than that

ROBBIE   we've t'see a guy t'day about readies or this place is fucked

IGGY   that's a bad situation that robbie / a didn't realize . . .

ROBBIE   doesn't matter what you realize – fuck all t'do with you / it's a business meetin – that's the point am makin / sometimes i might give the impression am not holdin it all t'gether / see me cowpted over that table ya might get the impression the war's over / i want you t'scrub the impression / is it scrubbed?

IGGY   scrubbed robbie

ROBBIE   the impression you now stick with is robbie the businessman / robbie the man with his head well an truly fuckin screwed on

IGGY   that's the way i see you robbie / yer a businessman – ya own this place / i respect that / i understan what yer sayin t'me

ROBBIE   respect / aye / changes need t'be made y'see / big changes / what's the difference between you an joe over there?

IGGY   am conscious

ROBBIE   very good / yer a very funny fella / that man has
readies / that man pays his way / thirteen years he's
been here – thirteen years he's paid his way / no
longer a fuckin dosshouse – y'see / ya wanna stay
here ya put yer hand in yer pocket – other than that
come closin time ya fuck off home / understan
what am sayin?

IGGY   it's all a bit haywire at the moment y'know / am
hangin aroun tryin t'get my napper t'gether – that's
what am doin

ROBBIE   yer not listenin t'me / robbie the drinker's heart
might bleed for ye – robbie the businessman
doesn't give a fuck / a few gargles t'day then yer
home

IGGY   a want t'do that / y'know – a mean / intendin t'do
that / a wanna go home / see her an the kids –
that's important / ya know yerself – ya drink yer
way through it – then ya go home / a know that –
don't think a don't know that

ROBBIE   drink yer drink

IGGY   should a phone her / think a should phone first /
look am nearly finished then am sailin home – type
a crack / she'll understan that – understandable
thing – that's why / should a phone her aye

ROBBIE   robbie the businessman / doesn't give a fuck

IGGY   right – thanks robbie / cheers

Vera enters from hotel with tea.

VERA   that pipe under the sink's leakin again

ROBBIE   have a look at it later

VERA   a plumber be the wrong thing wouldn't it / *to Iggy*
/ talkin about me was he – he does that / turn yer
back an his mouth opens

ROBBIE   don't flatter yerself dear – more important things /
explainin the ways of the world a was

IGGY   ways a the world – aye

VERA   that be somethin you'd know about to robbie

ROBBIE   it would vera that's correct / man a the world

VERA   big plans robbie an still stuck here / must be hard for ya is it

ROBBIE   the four corners a the earth dear – only a had you on my shirt tail

VERA   globetrotter / listen t'that / what colour's the buses?

ROBBIE   waitin on one this years t'take you away

VERA   the ones in t'town – what colour?

ROBBIE   bus colour

VERA   colour a yer eyes / red / travellin man / only for me yer head be in the gutter

ROBBIE   aye / no milk in this / forget that did ye / tell me this – what's the point in knowin the colour a buses if ya forget t'put milk in the fuckin tea

VERA   like the babycham robbie there is none / alec hasn't arrived with the goods yet

ROBBIE   not like 'im t'be late

VERA   he's not late / got another phonecall about 'im last night / too drunk t'tell ye ya were

ROBBIE   don't tell me now either / don't want t' know / whatever it is – leave me out

VERA   i'll deal with it will a / like everythin else roun this tip

ROBBIE   that's what that means / i say – a don't wanna know – that means – you deal with it

VERA   he threw another wobbler he did / chased the wardens or whatever thay are roun the place with a stick / locked them in a room – stacked up all the furniture then tried t'set fire t'it

ROBBIE   he's always at that crack / what?

VERA	a got the impression on the phone it was startin t'piss them off

Joe wakes.

IGGY	alright joe / everythin alright
JOE	still here?
IGGY	another day at the coalface joe – wha
JOE	aye
ROBBIE	alright kid
JOE	aye
VERA	breakfast not be long joe just waitin on alec with the bread an milk
ROBBIE	alec went . . .
JOE	a heard / talkin waken the dead it would
VERA	rested yer head upstairs you'd hear nothin
ROBBIE	would a not / alright vera aye
VERA	the joys a spring joe
IGGY	united's gonna sell their keeper joe / wanker he is
JOE	keeper? / keeper fuck
ROBBIE	that's right joe / more important things
VERA	listen t'me balloon head / what about alec?
ROBBIE	that's lovely innit / balloon head / lovely joe – wha
JOE	lovely
VERA	alec?
ROBBIE	alec's a balloon head / two balloon heads
IGGY	three
JOE	am in there
ROBBIE	four balloon heads vera
VERA	finished? / this is his last chance / one more thing an he's out – that's what they said / an accordin t'them – it's our fault

ROBBIE   our fuckin fault? / what way our fault?

VERA   what way / he sits up here an you fill 'im fulla
drink – that's what way

JOE   the man's entitled t'a few gargles / what else – a
mean – fuck he's entitled / has nothin

ROBBIE   i'm t'blame? / heap it all fuckin on there / backs
not broke yet

VERA   yer t'blame for everythin – ya know that robbie /
don't be hidin from it

ROBBIE   very good

VERA   t'blame for everythin joe

JOE   aye / the heap

ROBBIE   down in that kip he's in he gets fuck all / all the
do's feed 'im / don't give a fuck – the lock 'im out
the rest a the time / he comes up here – he gets
somethin t'do – a few odd jobs that half the time
don't need t'be fuckin done – a few pints for doin
them / they don't look after 'im we look after 'im /
an i'm t'fuckin blame / a don't think so / an don't
think a wont tell 'em that / burns a few sticks a
furniture – fuck / the place is a kip anyway

JOE   worse than alec there is

ROBBIE   that's right

VERA   he'll be through that door any second – sort it out
globetrotter

ROBBIE   the beautiful vera

*Alec enters from street carrying a bag of groceries
and a newspaper.*

ALEC   sunny day out there robbie / go out an get the sun
ya should

ROBBIE   sunny enough in here alec

ALEC   *puts groceries on counter and sets the newspaper
in front of Joe* / lizzy in the bakery was goin t'give

me the bill vera / bill t'morrow a told her / think
she'd know that vera / got a new watch / numbers /
lights up in the dark / no batteries though / lizzy
said she saw someone on the road / know who it
was robbie / jimmy mac / walkin she said – no car /
suit on 'im / new watch she said he had on 'im too /
not as good as my watch / maybe the give 'im a
watch in jail robbie

ROBBIE   aye / fucker / must've let 'im out

ALEC   let 'im out aye robbie

ROBBIE   bad fucker – alec / stay away from 'im

ALEC   he is robbie – jimmy mac's a bad fucker / good suit
            on 'im / no car / he's a bad fucker joe – isn't he

JOE   aye alec – bad fucker

VERA   robbie wants t'talk t'ya about somethin alec

ALEC   just talkin t'im there now vera / only jokin vera

ROBBIE   sit down alec

ALEC   have t'tidy up robbie

ROBBIE   leave that a minute

ALEC   can't leave it robbie – have t'do my work – get my
            lunch – go t'joes house – feed the cat – tidy up –
            have my tea – watch my programmes – cant leave
            it robbie

ROBBIE   you've time alec don't panic – sit down there

ALEC   a like havin a pint when am sittin down robbie

ROBBIE   pull 'im a pint

ALEC   pull us a pint vera

VERA   it's nine o'clock in the day an we're givin 'im a
            pint

ROBBIE   just pull 'im the fuckin thing

            *Iggy finishes what's in his glass and catches Vera's
            eye for another pint. Alec sits at a table. Robbie*

sits facing him. Joe puts some money on the
counter and pushes his empty glass towards Vera.

JOE   fire a tomato juice in that vera / take the edge of it

ROBBIE   alec

ALEC   robbie

ROBBIE   vera got a phonecall last night alec sayin that ya threw the head up again

ALEC   the don't like me down there robbie / talk about me when am asleep the do / the don't like me robbie / *Vera sets the pint down* / thank you vera / lizzy at the bakery vera – no sense

VERA   no sense – alec / this'll not be long joe

JOE   aye / give us a shout

Vera takes the groceries and exits to the hotel.

ROBBIE   member what ya were at last night alec?

ALEC   took t'my bed an the talked about me robbie / the don't like me robbie

ROBBIE   ya tried t'burn the kip down again alec

ALEC   no robbie – no

ROBBIE   listen t'what am sayin – ya did / understan? / ya did

ALEC   a did?

ROBBIE   ya did

ALEC   no / went t'my bed an the talked about me robbie

ROBBIE   ya come up here an ya do a bit a work – right?

ALEC   after this pint robbie / do my work then

ROBBIE   do yer work – have a few pints / that's it / no more nonsense alec ya understan / any more a that crack an ya can't come back here

ALEC   i'll stay here / the don't like me down there robbie

ROBBIE   ya can't stay here / this is a hotel / not like the kip yer in

ALEC   me an joe / joe stays here / me an joe'll stay here

JOE   ya wouldn't like it here alec / fuckin kip it is

ROBBIE   good enough for you / no more nonsense alec or ya
            can't come back

ALEC   have t'do my work

ROBBIE   jesus christ / behave yerself down there – an yer
            alright here / understan?

ALEC   understood robbie

ROBBIE   right / knock that in t'ya an away out an tidy the
            yard up / after that mop out the kitchen an finish
            off with takin a brush t'this place

            Alec finishes pint.

ALEC   money ready for the cat joe?

JOE   sort ya out before ya go

ALEC   sort me out before a go joe

            Alec exits to hotel.

ROBBIE   put yer head away that

JOE   he's hard goin

IGGY   he always like that?

ROBBIE   what ya mean from birth or what?

IGGY   aye

ROBBIE   no / postman was he? / milkman?

JOE   somethin like that / delivery or somethin / don't
            know

ROBBIE   doin his roun's / this is away at the start like –
            twenty years an more

JOE   would be that

ROBBIE   jumped out a car they did – shot 'im in the head
            an away / not right since / slowed 'im up y' know /
            couldn't repair whatever damage was done / said
            it wasn't him they were lookin for to – alec had

taken somebody elses shift or somethin / no good t'him that

IGGY   nice place – wha

ROBBIE   aye

          Vera enters from hotel.

VERA   that's ready joe

JOE   right ready now / *finishes his drink*

VERA   *to Robbie* / yer not sittin aroun / the pipe needs sortin then the books

ROBBIE   thank you for remindin me dear / fuckin order in the chaos ya are / when ya die am getting a plaque mounted out there let the world know what a martyr for yer cause ya were

VERA   assumin yer still aroun / crates of babycham take their toll a hear

JOE   *exiting to hotel* / the fry's the thing

IGGY   you'll be back in? / not leave me on my todd

JOE   later / cupla hours kip – get scrubbed up – fuck / *exits to hotel*

VERA   am goin up t'air the rooms / get rid a the stink

ROBBIE   worked its way up there has it / maybe there's a different type a stink up there

VERA   the pipe an the books / *exits to hotel*

ROBBIE   *finishes his tea* / cold tea / own a hotel an ya end up drinkin cold fuckin tea / *pours himself a drink and knocks it back* / there are advantages – not many – a few / you sittin here – aye

IGGY   nothin else for it

ROBBIE   member what a said – t'days home time / i'll be in next door – ya need a drink give me a shout / ya understan?

IGGY   aye robbie

ROBBIE   fixin pipes an cold tea – wha / *Robbie exits to hotel*

Iggy waits a moment then fills his glass from the pump. He watches the television.

Before lunch. Iggy, a few pints down the road, is still watching television. Joe is cleaned up and sitting in his usual seat, reading the paper. Robbie enters from hotel dressed in suit and tie etc. He carries a ledger.

ROBBIE   what any man woman or child needs t'know about the world of accounting an how it can be shaped into an art form is in this book / ya could mistake this place for the hilton if ya read it with a clear head / *pours himself a drink*

JOE   hilton alright

IGGY   if it's not right whoever it is'll know

ROBBIE   it is right / don't be talkin not right / right alright

VERA   *enters from hotel. Skirt suit – big blouse – make up.* / that the first one a day aye?

ROBBIE   first one – oh sweetness

VERA   credit where credit's due robbie / holdin out that long / what a man

ROBBIE   not many of us left dear

VERA   the book's done – he's goin t'what t'talk facts an figures y'know / this top man a yers

ROBBIE   everythin spot on / personal friend a mine the man is / he knows the score / a few gargles isn't gonna make the difference one way or the other

VERA   very professional / yer topman's gonna be impressed – no doubt

ROBBIE   i'm professional / don't ever say i'm not professional / a know what am at / impressed /

impressed all right / i'll show ya what he'll be
impressed about / *looks for something under the
counter* / where are they – you hide them?

VERA   oh jesus / where they always are / where they've
been for ever

ROBBIE   impressed / fuckin right / *rolls out a set of plans on
the counter* / what's that / you see these before?

JOE   as often as a shave

ROBBIE   aye / look at that

IGGY   what / what is it?

VERA   ya mean ya can't tell by lookin at it

ROBBIE   plans / that's what it is / impress people / *to Vera* /
haven't a clue what yer talkin about

IGGY   bit rough lookin robbie

ROBBIE   what would you know – rough lookin / plans they
are

JOE   rough plans

ROBBIE   that's correct / ya can have rough plans ya know –
they're allowed in the world

VERA   why are the plans rough robbie – tell 'im why
they're rough

ROBBIE   ya know nothin – this is technical / right – technical

VERA   technical / drew them when ya were pissed /
another top man a yers – used t'get pissed in here –
at some new pub in the town he was / both of ya's
pissed / he's tellin ya what it was like / he couldn't
speak – you couldn't write / jesus christ

ROBBIE   it was an arthitect a was talkin to / that man knew
what he was about

VERA   architect / you were there – what was he joe?

JOE   was he not an architect?

VERA   he designed kitchens – an by the look a him he was
fuckin useless at it

ROBBIE   architect he was / top man architect

VERA   robbie don't bring them – we'll look like fools

IGGY   can't make head nor tail a them – what's that?

ROBBIE   what's that / i'll tell ya what that is / that's whats gonna help turn this place aroun

IGGY   looks like a boat or ski run or somethin

VERA   it's a big – window

ROBBIE   two new gaffs down the road – what have they both got?

VERA   lots a people sittin in them havin a drink an enjoyin themselves

ROBBIE   big windows at the front / people can see in / they like that / they see in – so they go in

JOE   once they see in here they'll fuckin flood in / *puts money on the counter. Vera gets him a drink*

ROBBIE   done up the would / wood an all that caper / pillars / booths / lovely big window – let the light in / belfast's changin isn't it / the keep sayin it's changin – so it must be fuckin changin / this place is changin / places down the road are fuckin kips / this place be like the way it was before

          Alec enters from hotel.

ALEC   the kitchen's all mopped out robbie / will a brush up now robbie?

ROBBIE   aye alec you do that / the likes a that fucker jimmy mac gets a new start the same goes for us

ALEC   *brushing up* / jimmy mac's a fucker robbie

ROBBIE   aye alec

VERA   how's it goin t'be different this time

ROBBIE   different times that's why

VERA   what happened with the compensation money – you forget that

ROBBIE   what happened / you tell me what happened

VERA   i'll tell ya all right / it was alright up t'that point –
an sometimes alright can be good enough / ya
drank nearly every penny of it robbie / that there's
somethin here at all's only down t'me / change /
join the gravytrain / remortgage / get us back t'the
good times / drank that to robbie / ya know what /
a probably wouldn't've minded but there weren't
even good times in the drinkin of it

ROBBIE   you had good times all right / and plenty of them

VERA   you stick t'yer top men an those fuckin plans there
/ we'll see how that goes will we

ROBBIE   we'll try an work somethin out with yer network a
friends will we / not too many on that list is there

VERA   plenty on it before a met you / am goin out t'turn
the car / *gives joe the keys to the hotel* / we're not
expectin anybody

JOE   aye

VERA   there wont be but if anybody wanders in off the
street lookin lunch tell the chef had to leave to sign
copies of his latest book – what i cooked for the
rich an famous – but he left some sandwiches in
the kitchen / i've a feelin this isn't goin t'take long
anyway joe

ROBBIE   it'll take as long as any other business meetin

VERA   don't be long

    Vera exits to hotel.

ROBBIE   she's some performer – wha / *pours himself a drink
– watches the television* / charlton heston dead?

IGGY   the actor?

ROBBIE   no charlton heston the fuckin deep sea diver / yes
the fuckin actor

IGGY   don't know

ROBBIE   on the news yesterday he was

JOE	head a the gun lobby in america
ROBBIE	didn't know that
JOE	ben hur was a good movie
ROBBIE	aye / better go out here / alright there?
JOE	aye
ROBBIE	joe there might be a guy weigh in from the brewery / a don't think he will but he might / it's nothin – just tell 'im a had t'rush out – personal business / in fact keep 'im here – give 'im a drink i'll sort 'im out when a get back
JOE	aye / should get paid for this y'know
ROBBIE	aren't ya always in my thoughts – that's payment enough / alright alec?
ALEC	alright robbie
ROBBIE	member what a said now / take it easy t'day
ALEC	take it easy robbie
ROBBIE	aye

Robbie exits to hotel with plans and ledger.

JOE	think it was me owned this kip
IGGY	could a won somethin
JOE	who?
IGGY	charlton heston
JOE	ben hur a good movie

Alec finishes brushing up.

ALEC	finished now joe / need the keys an the money for the cat joe / cold turkey for the cat / do that this afternoon after lunch joe
JOE	*gives Alec keys and money* / tidy over there is it?
ALEC	tidy joe / all the rubbish in the wheelie bin
JOE	best place for it alec

ALEC   best place for it joe

JOE   wanna wee one – start ya off

ALEC   a wee one aye joe

Alec sits down. Joe gets him a drink.

IGGY   what's the crack here when they're not about – we just wang away at the gargle buckshee?

JOE   no / you've a drink in front a ye – worry about the next one when ya have none

Alec downs his drink.

ALEC   am away for my lunch now joe / eat first work later – joe

JOE   good luck alec

Alec exits to street.

IGGY   you a house?

JOE   aye – big one across the way there

IGGY   ya never said / three days talkin ya never said

JOE   a lot a things a don't say

IGGY   the house – is it empty like?

JOE   aye

IGGY   don't get that / a mean – what – why don't ya live in it

JOE   don't want to

IGGY   what's yer man tidyin up if it's empty?

JOE   nothin / feeds the cat / sits there / a don't know what he does / don't care what he does

IGGY   you check up now an again like or what

JOE   a just told ye a don't go near it

IGGY   furniture in it – aye

JOE   everythin in it / same as the day a left it

IGGY   a don't get this

JOE	sit an drink yer pint
IGGY	not like talkin about it
JOE	that's right
IGGY	we're sittin here y'know
JOE	an wha?
IGGY	more to it than getting pissed or whatever / talkin / findin out about people an stuff / what they're about / fuck a don't know – just – talkin t'each other
JOE	you do nothin but talk / every damn thing under the sun – talkin about it
IGGY	it touches me – everythin touches me / the world – the whole lot – the big picture / it touches me
JOE	aye / touched
IGGY	if a've been doin all the talkin it's yer turn now
JOE	a don't like talkin
IGGY	tell us
JOE	a just said
IGGY	a know what ya just said / tell us
JOE	my wife fucked off / right / that's it
IGGY	cause a the drink like or what
JOE	no / she just left
IGGY	an what?
JOE	an nothin
IGGY	the house / what's the crack with the house?
JOE	after she took off a didn't set foot in the house again / didn't feel right / just didn't feel right
IGGY	what ya call her?
JOE	ruby / see where am sittin here – that's where she use t'sit / her seat / *finishes his drink and pours himself another one* / ya want one a these / it's paid for

IGGY   not good with shorts – y'know

JOE   up t'yerself

IGGY   ah fuck it – give us one

Joe pours Iggy a drink.

JOE   good luck

IGGY   aye

JOE   the two a us used t'come here – ruby an me / more
life about it then / house across the way – handy /
she'd come in on her own some a the time y'know
/ a wee vodka / sit here an talk t'robbie / him an
her got on well y'know / talk t'anybody she would
/ good company / she was known for that – known
for bein good company / most a the time she'd do
my talkin for me / works like that sometimes / yer
one type they're another / fits / makes sense / feels
right or somethin – a don't know / she would never
light the fire / all the time we were t'gether never
once lit the fire or went out t'the yard t'get coal /
she said that was a mans job / used t'joke with her
that in another life she must a been in a coal minin
disaster – an that's why she wouldn't go near it /
we were meant t'go out t'gether this night / me an
ruby an robbie an vera / didn't go out that often or
anythin / enough goin on here – y'know / goin out
to a brewery do we were / they were presentin
robbie with somethin – a don't know – best run
pub or somethin like that / he invited me an ruby /
one a those ones ya get dressed up for it was /
always gotta look yer best / a was the only one not
ready / come straight in here from work – did that
sometimes / all in good form the were / i just sat
on – wasn't thinkin about getting dressed up an
that / come the time t'go i had t'shoot over t'the
house an fire the suit on me an that / robbie says
the couldn't be late in case he missed his big
moment / he wanted ruby t'go with them an me
meet them there / i was fine with that – big do's
aren't my – y'know / ruby said she'd sit here an

wait on me / that was that / the two a them took off
in a taxi / i went t'put my suit on an left her here /
a was havin a shave / we've all got used t'hearin
blasts but this one would've burst yer ears open /
knew it was this place / runnin over here thought a
was goin t'throw up / place was crazy / dust / bits a
things everywhere / bits a people / couldn't find her
/ screamin her name a was / couldn't think where
t'look / didn't want t'look for fear of findin
somethin / then she just walked out in t'the street /
slow motion / she just walked out an stood there –
didn't know what she was lookin at / blood all over
her arms / didn't speak / just held her / no injuries –
blood must a been somebody else's / said at the
hospital that she was in shock / felt like sayin tell
me somethin a don't know / the said that different
people handle it differently an it was just a matter
a time / hang in there an it'll sort itself out type a
thing / she never spoke about it / hardly talked at
all / just waited / few weeks later a came in from
work this night an she was gone / packed her stuff
an just left / left a note sayin she was sorry but she
had t'go an wouldn't be back / haven't seen her
since / funny thing to / see that cat alec feeds – it
arrived from nowhere the day she left / tiny wee
kitten / funny fuckin thing that / waited / spendin
most a my time here anyway so a just moved in /
haven't been back over the road since / *he takes a
drink and pours himself another one*

IGGY   fucked up place it is / what ya think she's doin or
            what – or where or anythin

JOE   i never tell that story – right / a don't want no more
            talk about it / understan what am sayin?

IGGY   ya still love her like?

JOE   a just said no more / right

IGGY   right / not right like is it / think a might phone my
            wife / let her know what the crack is an that
            y'know

JOE   go home

IGGY   phone her first / always better t'phone first it is

JOE   aye / *finishes his drink* / am goin t'go out an sit in
             reception in case this guy from the brewery weighs
             in – make the place a bit more respectable lookin

IGGY   i'll sit out there with ye

JOE   no i'll sit on my own / read the paper

IGGY   aye – sure i'll be on the phone t'her anyway

             *Joe folds his newspaper and exits to hotel. Iggy
             finishes his vodka and pours himself another one.
             He leans over the counter and pulls himself a pint
             as well. He settles down to watch the television.*

*After lunch. Iggy is in the same position watching the
television. He drinks the last of his pint.*

IGGY   news fuck / took ya three days t'ride somewhere
             t'say it – make sure then it wasn't a lot a shite /
             rich people in love an starvin babies lyin on the
             groun – aye / that's the message – now we're gettin
             there / the money message / two points up against
             the yak yak of outer fuckin do dah / we're in deep
             shit now

             *Joe enters from hotel with a tray of tea and
             sandwiches.*

IGGY   we're in deep shit now / we're up two points or
             down two points against the yo yo bin bin chats

JOE   dow jones

IGGY   aye him too

JOE   there's tea in that / have a sandwich – brewery guy
             wasn't hungry

IGGY   not now / too late now

JOE	*pours a cup of tea* / not goin t'believe this / know what the brewery guys name was
IGGY	double vodka
JOE	close / joe beer / that's who he is – he's joe beer the brewery man / hows about that – wha
IGGY	aye names are all up the left / listen t'this – this is important / important this is / this come on the tv about two pints ago
JOE	pay for them aye
IGGY	aye a paid for them / listen t'this / some woman went t'some oliver hardy an wore this dress chat / shiny chats / wouldn't be my – y'know my trick / too glitzy / my wife not go for that type a thing / plain chats / this dress – must a cost a fuckin fortune too / this dress had no arse in it – an yer women wasn't wearin any trunks / ya could see her jamroll
JOE	need t'watch what ya'd be sittin on
IGGY	thought that / newspaper be bad – print
JOE	plastic
IGGY	that be cat too / don't get me wrong here she had a good jamroll / the point am makin is what the fuck y'know / it's up there – it's on the fuckin screen / there's punters in countries with fuck all runnin about in the nip all the fuckin time – dyin / have fuck all / an it's news like that some brass nail has a hole in her fuckin dress – know what a mean / somethin fuckin wrong about that like
JOE	don't watch it then
IGGY	it's there – have t'watch it
JOE	don't talk about it then
IGGY	what's the point in watchin it if ya don't fuckin talk about it
JOE	a don't know / television – don't care

IGGY	we should care
JOE	aye
IGGY	we should care but we don't that's the point am makin
JOE	you've made it – right / *checks his watch* / alec be back soon for the afternoon shift
IGGY	over in the house is he aye
JOE	should be – bring the mail back with 'im
IGGY	aye / there's somethin a want t'talk t'ya about / ask ya somethin
JOE	what ya lookin – tenner – score?
IGGY	not that no – not that / maybe get that off ya later like – not now though
JOE	what?
IGGY	am goin home
JOE	now?
IGGY	no no not now / make a phonecall first / t'day sometime / t'night maybe – whatever / am goin home – that's that right / but say just in case a don't / say somethin happens maybe / don't know what the score is about ye y'know / might be home t'morrow instead a t'day / robbie's a gentleman / vera's a good woman – lovely woman / let me kip here anytime – that's soun / am not sayin there will be but there might be a problem there or somethin – a don't know / maybe vera or somethin – talkin a wee bit fuckin funny she is / could all go belly up y'know / if that's the situation / if that's the way it goes / is there / is there any chance i could kip down in that house a yers / empty house across the way
JOE	no
IGGY	no?
JOE	aye no

IGGY   but a mean – it's lyin there

JOE   that's our house / no body stays there

IGGY   our house?

JOE   yes our house

IGGY   right / only askin y'know

JOE   ya asked an ya got yer answer

IGGY   you should sell it / get the readies for it / sell it / price a houses roun here up through the fuckin roof

JOE   are the

Robbie enters from the hotel. He doesn't look as smart as he did a few hours ago. He puts his plans and ledger on the counter.

IGGY   yer a gentleman robbie

ROBBIE   still here? / time you were off a think

IGGY   still here robbie – still here / headin off soon

JOE   well?

ROBBIE   no

JOE   brewery man weighed in

ROBBIE   fuck / what?

JOE   not a happy man robbie / waited as long as he could / left his card – phone 'im immediately he says

ROBBIE   fuck 'im he can join the queue / a need t'have a word with ye about somethin

JOE   wha?

ROBBIE   not now – she's in behind me / later – not now / don't be mentionin the brewery guy t'her

JOE   right

Vera enters from street. She slams the front door shut. She sits at the counter – nobody speaks. She gets up and walks behind the bar.

VERA   i'm gonna have a drink / *she pours herself a drink*) / anybody else? / robbie? / don't let me down robbie

ROBBIE   aye why not

VERA   babycham?

ROBBIE   no

VERA   nearly forgot / stupid bitch / all out a babycham / iggy? / joe? / a drink? / it's on the house / on our house

JOE   am alright

IGGY   aye – why not / it's all mapped out now anyway

VERA   *lifts plans and ledger* / put these away will a / somewhere safe / wouldn't want anybody stealin them / put them down here?

ROBBIE   you do that vera

VERA   *pouring* / is that enough in that? / ya can have more / it's alright t'have more

ROBBIE   that's plenty

VERA   ya sure joe / yer welcome to it

JOE   i've tea here – take one later vera not now / keys / *Joe hands Vera the hotel keys and she puts them in her handbag.*

VERA   anythin excitin happen joe when we were away?

JOE   not that a noticed vera no

VERA   nothing exciting?

JOE   no

         Vera sits beside Iggy.

VERA   *finishes her drink* / another one a those please / know what i think?

ROBBIE   no what?

VERA   i think we should all just sit here an get pissed / bit of a change / you game for that iggy?

IGGY   i'm yer man

VERA   *handed drink* / thank you darling

ROBBIE   yer welcome sweetness

VERA   get pissed / so no news then boys

IGGY   the world's up the fuckin left an there's a woman
            runnin roun the place with no arse in her dress / if
            ya were goin out of a night vera would ya wear
            somethin like that

VERA   would depend on what mood a was in

IGGY   wee lads in our street had no arse in their trousers
            – that's different though

VERA   a have the body for it / what do ya think iggy –
            would a have the body for it?

IGGY   certainly ya would

VERA   joe / still have it enough t'flash a bit a flesh

JOE   turn a few heads vera

VERA   stomachs a think joe not heads / what do ya think –
            will a get one a those dresses robbie / flash a bit a
            flesh / you like that? / a could wear it pullin pints /
            yer big window – everyone see me – get all the
            punters in / what ya think robbie – that be a bit of a
            turn on would it? / right it's decided – am gonna
            cut the arse out a all my dresses / start now / get
            me the scissors

ROBBIE   *hands her scissors* / here

VERA   what way would ya go about this / do it yerself job
            / *she stands up, bends over and looks through her
            legs* / think this is the way the woman on the box
            did it / no / *stands up* / have t'take it off / *her back
            to Iggy* / unzip me / unzip me – come on / you've
            unzipped plenty a them before am sure

IGGY   only talkin a lot a nonsense vera / don't be cuttin
            yer clothes up

VERA   *her back to joe* / joe / do the business joe

JOE   ya gonna get me that vodka now

VERA   he'll get it – get joe a vodka / no takers then / no
             point in askin you / *sits down* / useless / a hear
             united's sellin their keeper / wanker he is from
             what a can gather

ROBBIE   united who vera

VERA   united with the wanker keeper / yous are no fun /
             need somewhere with a bit a fun / energy / light /
             we need light robbie / *finishes her drink* / i'm goin
             down the road t'have a drink where there's light /
             no point in askin the old ones / ya want t'come
             with me iggy? / stay here too long ya turn t'stone

IGGY   am settled here vera y'know

VERA   don't worry i've money on me / what are ya lookin
             at him for / am askin you t'have a drink with me /
             two adults havin a drink / no need t'look at him /
             robbie doesn't mind / wouldn't matter if he did /
             you don't mind do ya robbie / iggy an i go for a
             wee drink somewhere brighter

ROBBIE   do whatever ya want vera

VERA   do whatever ya want vera / see / let's go

             They finish their drinks.

IGGY   we'll not be long

VERA   we'll be as long as we want / you can look after
             things robbie i'll doubt there'll be a rush

             *Iggy and Vera exit to street. Robbie pours himself a
             drink and sits beside Joe.*

ROBBIE   got off lightly there – wha

JOE   more maybe

ROBBIE   aye

JOE   not work out no?

ROBBIE   fuck / not work out / what is it ya gotta do / a don't
             know / fuckin wearin me down it is joe / am sittin

waitin on this fuckin head the ball arrivin / vera's
givin it all that / understan'able – still doesn't
make it easy t'listen to / sittin lookin at all the
punters in the place we are / nice gaff / good shape
of a counter / not like this fuckin thing / went roun
in a bend / ya could be standin at it an there could
still be plenty a room – know that way / sittin
thinkin fuck this am goin t'do a runner here / go sit
on a wall someplace an watch the world pass by /
wish t'fuck a had a / have t'pull yerself t'gether
don't ye

JOE   nothin else for it

ROBBIE   ya reckon?

JOE   sometimes – other times no

ROBBIE   a was lookin at the barman pullin a pint / kept
             thinkin i used t'enjoy doin that / not brain surgery
             but – a simple thing done well or somethin like that /
             thought t'myself i could enjoy doin that again /
             then head the ball danders in / haven't seen ye for a
             while – blah blah – old times – all that / knew right
             away / this is my last roll a the dice an this guy's
             turned in t'a fuckin balloon / didn't say anythin
             t'her like / she knew anyway – seen enough a them
             about this place / it was like ya knew it wasn't goin
             t'work out but ya hoped it might so ya carry on
             with it / it was like that / went along with it / talkin
             t'me like a stranger he was / everythin was gonna
             be easy know that way

JOE   if everythin was easy we'd all be at it

ROBBIE   correct / all telephone numbers / not interested in
             plans or books or fuck all – just telephone numbers /
             talkin about openin offices all over the show he is /
             am tryin t'explain the situation t'im / he's all new
             start – new this – everythin's possible / sayin how
             we all need t'tap in t'this new foun energy /
             investigate the new opportunities available / nothin
             / the guy's a fuckin joker / can't do anythin for us /

might be able t'do somethin if we have collatoral /
i explained we don't that's why we're here / can't
help – would love t'help but can't / another double
napper tandy / dead cert / then he starts in t'it /
lost everythin – wife – kids – house – business /
gamblin / tryin t'pull himself t'gether – tryin t'start
up again / we were gonna be his first clients /
thought he could do it but he can't / doesn't understan why – he just can't / couldn't stop apologisin
t'us / must've a big sign roun my fuckin do a /
he's leavin – what does he do / trys t'tap me for
a fuckin tenner / i'd a fuckin slapped 'im only he
looked too stupid

Alec enters from street.

ALEC   alright joe

JOE   any letters for me over there alec?

ALEC   no letters t'day joe

JOE   nothin

ALEC   nothin joe

JOE   all tidy are wa

ALEC   all tidy joe

ROBBIE   have ya nothin t'be at alec – we're tryin t'have a
          conversation here

ALEC   talk away robbie i'll just sit here

ROBBIE   a don't want ye sittin there at the moment that's
          what am sayin

JOE   man's been graftin hard all day – allowed t'settle
          he is / normally back before this alec – some
          grafter ya are

ALEC   i've done somethin

JOE   done somethin what way?

ALEC   must a done somethin – but a didn't do anythin

ROBBIE   talk right alec

ALEC   did everythin the same / everythin the same as
          always joe / tidy up / cold turkey in the catdish /
          pish wish wish wish / no cat joe / all roun the
          place – everywhere joe – it's not there / didn't do
          anythin different joe / didn't lose it joe – just not
          there

ROBBIE   calm down alec son

ALEC   joes cat robbie

JOE   give 'im a pint / ya want a pint?

ALEC   aye joe a pint

ROBBIE   have a pint later alec not now

JOE   he's upset for fuck sake – give 'im the pint

ALEC   never lost before / everyday there / never lost
          before

JOE   alec – alec – it's alright / it's nothin t'do with you
          don't worry about it

ALEC   nothin t'do with me joe that's right / nobody better
          touch it joe – i'll fuckin kill them / fuckin kill them
          a will

JOE   it was an old cat alec

ALEC   it was an old cat joe

ROBBIE   here

ALEC   *pint* / cheers robbie / thanks robbie – cheers / it
          was an old cat joe

JOE   probably away t'die somewhere alec – that's what
          they do / don't they do that robbie

ROBBIE   oh aye away t'die / knock that in t'ya alec / sunny
          day away out for a dander or somethin

ALEC   rather sit here robbie / give us somethin t'do

ROBBIE   there is nothin for ya t'do

ALEC   tidy up the stairs

ROBBIE   yer not allowed near the rooms ya know that

ALEC   just sit here then robbie

ROBBIE   fuck / *gives Alec money* / buy a carryout an sit
            outside there with it

ALEC   never see me drinkin in the street robbie / never see
            me drinkin in the street joe

JOE   nah alec

ALEC   buy batteries for my watch an radio / listen t'my
            radio at night robbie

ROBBIE   aye do that

ALEC   don't look for the cat joe

JOE   no point alec

ALEC   *finishes pint* / back later robbie / listen t'my radio –
            have my tea – back later

            Alec exits to street.

JOE   that cat arrived the day ruby left – know that

ROBBIE   aye a know it – course a know it – an wha?

JOE   nothin – just sayin / strange like

ROBBIE   everythin alright?

JOE   what ya mean alright / aye / alright aye

ROBBIE   a need t'talk t'ya / just makin sure yer head's
            t'gether that's all / serious ya know / focused –
            know what am sayin

JOE   stop talkin like that / say whatever ya got a say

ROBBIE   ya know what am goin t'say / only got one thing to
            say / you know what it is

JOE   do a

ROBBIE   ya want another drink?

JOE   aye / *drinks poured* / you payin for that?

ROBBIE   aye am payin for it

JOE   put the readies in the till then

ROBBIE   fuck the till – sort that out later

JOE   have t'look after business

ROBBIE   this is what am doin now – right – am lookin after business / just think about this / it's about the house

JOE   aye the house

ROBBIE   other times we discussed this it's just been talk / this is more than talk – right / just listen / that's all am askin ya t'do at the moment – just listen / the house is lyin empty / understan why

JOE   do ye?

ROBBIE   you've been here all this while / it's lyin there / i understan – fuckin right i understan

JOE   right

ROBBIE   for whatever reasons – an ya know them / it's down t'me a understan that / t'day was the last – fuckin / the last outside way a goin about this / a've nowhere else t'go / the house is lyin there / yer house is lyin there

JOE   ruby an i's house

ROBBIE   ruby an yer house / this could happen / it could be somethin made happen / a few ways a doin this / go t'the bank – no more fuckin head the balls involved in this / straight t'the right people / use the house as collatoral – get the readies fire it in t'place / have this place the way it should be / fuck those kips down the road / that's the one way / the other way would be t'sell it / get more readies i'd say / wouldn't need t'fire everythin in t'this place – keep some readies for yerself / you could buy in t'this place / i'd sell ya a whack of it – become a partner / ya live here anyway – so a mean / be handy / get a good feelin sittin here – when the place is buzzin an that – knowin you own some of it / or if ya didn't want that type a hassle – wouldn't be any hassle cause i'd be coverin that /

ya didn't want the hassle ya could just lend me the money / pay ya back whatever a bank would pay ya back / all a this is solid / business / not just talk joe / another level – know what am sayin / understan there's punters say friends shouldn't get involved in this type a set up / that wouldn't be a problem with me an you / too long in the tooth / been down too many roads for anythin not right t'happen / it's a goldmine like / a real – y'know / fuckin goldmine it is / ya know that anyway / there's no point in me sayin the – ya know that

JOE   aye

ROBBIE   aye / i owe vera / whatever an all she does – i owe her / a can't fuck this up / this is about money an business / ya don't have t'say anythin now / a want ya t'think about it / you think about it?

JOE   aye / you've told me so a know what we're talkin about / i'll think about it / now's not the time for me t'be dealin with it / other things involved / not now

ROBBIE   understan joe – but you'll think about it

JOE   aye robbie a just said

ROBBIE   we'll not talk about it any more / it's said – it's done / you'll think about it / don't be mentionin anythin t'her about it

JOE   not mention anythin

ROBBIE   no point in her knowin anythin at this stage

JOE   right / no more

ROBBIE   think about it / finished / *looks at television* / camilla parker bowles

JOE   aye / some woman

ROBBIE   aye / earn their readies easy the do / a may go an phone this brewery guy – money he's lookin / the quiz men be in soon – ya sittin there

JOE   might dander down an get the late paper – maybe get somethin t'eat / ya want me t'sit here until they weigh in?

ROBBIE   aye / a want t'get this done now / don't want t'be phonin later with the gargle in me / give us a shout

JOE   aye

ROBBIE   fuckin tired am

JOE   long oul day alright

Robbie exits to hotel with tea tray.

After the quiz. Robbie is clearing pint glasses from one of the tables. Joe is reading the evening paper.

ROBBIE   did you know greenland was owned by denmark?

JOE   a did

ROBBIE   waste a brains that isn't it like / know the answers t'everythin an not a fuckin job among them

JOE   passes the time for them

ROBBIE   *behind the bar washing glasses* / ya need somethin t'fill it alright / if the bought more gargle it be better though / sittin over a pint half the day / in days gone by joe i'd a turfed them out on their arse

JOE   aye

ROBBIE   greenland an denmark a didn't know that / it's the type a thing that's hardly worth knowin though

JOE   better off knowin it than not knowin it

ROBBIE   that could be true / yer man asks the questions says he might try an get it off the groun at night / charge people in / he keeps the door i get the readies off the drink / that's if there is any drink / brewery man says they don't get paid soon they're goin t'stop deliverin / ya hear me?

JOE   a hear ye

ROBBIE   yer man asks the questions says that kip down the
             road has it goin at night / big crowds at it / prize
             money an that / *pours himself a drink* / ya want
             one a these?

JOE   aye

             *Robbie pours Joe a drink, pays for it then sits
             beside him at the counter.*

ROBBIE   made any decisions about what a said earlier?

JOE   no

ROBBIE   still thinkin about it?

JOE   still thinkin about it

ROBBIE   these things take time / not too much time but they
             take time

JOE   aye

ROBBIE   a was goin go in an make somethin t'eat – don't
             think i'll bother now / you had somethin – aye

JOE   when a was down the road earlier / stew

ROBBIE   any good?

JOE   alright – could a been hotter

             Alec enters from street carrying a suitcase.

ROBBIE   nice an slow – here we go / alright alec

ALEC   alright robbie aye / alright joe / do yer talkin
             robbie?

ROBBIE   aye alec

             Alec sits down. Silence.

ALEC   jimmy mac's a fucker robbie

ROBBIE   why's that alec?

ALEC   you said he was / i knew he was anyway / i knew
             he was robbie

ROBBIE   what's the suitcase for alec? / better not be what a think it is

ALEC   the don't like me down there robbie / joe the don't like me down there

ROBBIE   yer not stayin here / it's not a dosshouse alec / you can wicker about tidy up – fine / but yer not stayin here

ALEC   *puts money on the counter* / give us a pint robbie / alright joe / didn't come back joe / cat didn't come back

JOE   no

ALEC   beauty she was / not get another one like it / big fat cat full a cold turkey

ROBBIE   drink that alec then maybe another then yer back down the road

ALEC   can't go back robbie / out ya go the said

ROBBIE   i'll get vera t'phone them / she'll sort it out – it'll be alright

ALEC   no robbie no

ROBBIE   what no robbie no?

ALEC   jimmy macs watch / a belter / swap the watches / mines a beauty robbie look / look joe a beauty it is

JOE   it is alec a beauty

ALEC   said i was a mad man / said my watch was shite he did / good watch / hit 'im a did robbie / jimmy mac's a fucker

ROBBIE   a dig ya hit 'im?

ALEC   hit 'im a few times robbie / bust his face / bust his face open a did robbie / played football we did when we were kids / house across the street / jimmy mac lived in the house across the street robbie / his big brother used t'let me have a go on his bike / up along the river / peddlin the bike up along the river / drivin the car / him drivin the car

robbie / didn't say no / jimmy macs a fucker / bust
his face open / the don't like me down there robbie

ROBBIE   drink yer pint there alec / forget about all that alec
/ right

ALEC   forget about it robbie

ROBBIE   somethin be sorted out / always sort somethin out
alec

ALEC   somethin always sorted out robbie

ROBBIE   *to Joe* / what ya do about that / name a fuck / a
mean – I can't – fuck y'know

*Vera and Iggy enter from street. It's obvious
they've been drinking. Alec watches the television.*

ALEC   put on who wants t'be a millionaire robbie / like
that show / put it on robbie

Robbie changes stations. Vera sits at the bar.

VERA   sit down iggy / a know this isn't the type a kip
we're accustomed to but sit down anyway / *he sits
beside her* / who wants t'be a millionaire – i do

ALEC   it's a good show vera – yer man's good

VERA   good show alec / did you miss me robbie?

ROBBIE   my heart bled vera / countin every second a was

VERA   *looking in her handbag for money* / one last drink /
gonna have one last drink with everybody / (*puts
money on counter*) / get the boy wonder a pint /
alec – joe / everyone – get them all a drink / and
you the light of my life a want you t'have a drink
with me

Robbie gets drinks etc.

ALEC   c / it's c joe – isn't it c

JOE   c – aye / fuck it / don't know / might be a

IGGY   b it is

VERA   loved it down there robbie ya would've / all laid
           out lovely / an the people – beautiful / not
           scumbags / all top men – yer type a people they are

ROBBIE   glad you enjoyed yerself

VERA   oh yes – top notch people

ALEC   a

IGGY   should be b

ALEC   it's a

VERA   packed t'the doors the place was / must be makin a
           fortune robbie / bringin the money t'the bank in
           wheelbarrows the must be / all in wee uniforms /
           professional place / professional – that would be
           the word

ROBBIE   why don't ya get a job down there / woman a yer
           vast experience – all be out with open arms / *hands
           her a drink*

VERA   an you know it too / one last drink / hey iggy – one
           last drink

IGGY   aye aye – last drink aye

VERA   cheers robbie

ROBBIE   good luck vera

ALEC   d / it's d joe isn't it / d it is

JOE   d

IGGY   b again

VERA   have t'go now

ROBBIE   away t'yer bed aye

VERA   bed / no no no no / somethin t'do / have somethin
           t'do robbie / *to Iggy* / finish yer pint / i'll be back
           in a minute

           Vera exits to hotel.

ALEC   d joe / a told ya it was d / a said d joe

JOE   yer the man alec / millionaire

IGGY   robbie we have t' – have t'talk here

ROBBIE   drink yer pint an watch the t.v.

IGGY   don't be getting the wrong – the wrong notion here
            / gonna say somethin t'help ya out / makin it clear
            it's nothin t'do with me – right / all i was doin was
            talkin an havin a gargle

ROBBIE   what?

ALEC   d again joe / it's d again

JOE   an the man says d

IGGY   am blitzed here right / head's startin t'go a wee bit
            / still tellin ya somethin though / i like you / know
            what am sayin / i like you that's why I'm sayin this

ROBBIE   i don't like you

IGGY   ya don't know me

ROBBIE   i don't want t'know ya

IGGY   ya don't – y'know / this is the fucked up side / an
            alright side too / there is / anyway / vera was talkin
            a wee bit strange down there / nothin t'do with me
            – her it was / kept wantin t'talk about leavin /
            leavin for good like / sayin she had enough an all
            that type a chat / don't know what she's up t'now
            like / just tellin ya this / don't agree with her leavin
            by the way – that's wrong – shouldn't fuckin leave
            / people should stick with it regardless a what the
            fuck's goin on / she kept talkin about me goin with
            her / don't know where she got that from now / not
            from me right / happily married i am / phone her –
            have t'phone her / a just want t'wire ya off in case
            any – y'know / drunk she is / all be forgotten about
            whenever y'know

ALEC   b / has t'be b joe

JOE   aye

IGGY   maybe you should speak t'her or somethin / not
            right that she wants t'leave is it / flowers or
            somethin know what a mean / i do that type a
            crack / that's what i'm like / flowers an that sort it
            out / so that's what am sayin

ROBBIE   that it?

IGGY   that's what am sayin / that's it

ROBBIE   sure we'll see what happens / don't you panic
            about it / she gets a wee bit like that now an again

IGGY   woman wha

ROBBIE   aye

ALEC   b / am good joe / am good

JOE   get you on it alec / win a fortune

ALEC   a fortune joe aye

            Vera enters from hotel with a suitcase.

IGGY   robbie what am . . . .

ROBBIE   say nothin

VERA   robbie

ROBBIE   yes dear

IGGY   vera don't be / a was just sayin t'robbie..

VERA   iggy you don't have t'say anythin / it's not up t'you
            / i'll do the talkin / it's my resposibility

IGGY   that's what am sayin / don't be . . . .

ROBBIE   let her say what she has t'say – right

IGGY   right right right

ALEC   c / it's c this time joe

JOE   in yer head alec – not out loud

ALEC   *whispers* / c it is joe

VERA   finish yer pint iggy – then we can phone a taxi /
            i'm leavin robbie / we're leavin / don't be blamin
            iggy / these things just happen / just leavin – don't

want a scene / be decent that way robbie / i've had enough / enough is enough / can't grow old here / wasted too much bloody time here as it is / not that you care / i'm goin away robbie with another person t'start over again / a don't want a scene so we're just gonna leave / i've had enough – that's all there is to it robbie – i've had enough / we'll walk down an get a taxi iggy – i want t'go now / ya don't have t'say anythin robbie / a don't want ya t'say anythin / iggy

ROBBIE   you do what ya have t'do vera

VERA   *hands Robbie the keys of the hotel* / you'll be needin these

ROBBIE   aye

VERA   iggy come on

IGGY   this is all the drink talkin here / it's the drink talkin vera

VERA   don't be worried about him / it's nothin t'do with him / he doesn't care / come on let's go

IGGY   a don't know what – robbie

VERA   what ya talkin t'him for / fuck him / we're goin so come on

IGGY   sit down will ye – sit down

VERA   a don't want t'sit down / finish the damn drink an we'll go

IGGY   robbie a said / didn't a say / vera am not goin anywhere / jesus christ all a was doin was talkin t'ya y'know / fuck sake / i'm married for fuck sake / i love my wife / mightn't know that but a love her / a said this / robbie didn't a say this

VERA   you make him say that / you made him say it didn't ya

ROBBIE   he told me you were actin a bit strange vera that's all

VERA   fucker / iggy listen – i know he's told you t'say all
            that

IGGY   told me nothin

VERA   he's a bad bastard / he wants t'torture me / that's
            what he's doin – torturin me / he doesn't love me /
            you fucker / he loves someone he can't have an
            he's fuckin torturin me because of it / i've t'watch
            him day after day drink every drop a manhood out
            a himself / nothin works / he drank himself so
            nothin works / does it on purpose – fucker / you
            said t'me ya wanted t'go so we'll go / don't listen
            t'him / i can't stay here / don't listen t'the fucker

IGGY   i'm just havin a drink that's all am doin / i'm not
            goin anywhere – just havin a gargle

VERA   *to Robbie* / useless fuckin bastard / pisspot useless
            fucker / fucker / you fucker / phone my own taxi /
            my taxi to take me – take me / *she moves to the*
            phone at the end of the bar and rummages through
            her handbag for a phone number. She can't find it
            but dials anyway / nine – o – six / nine – o – six /
            she smashes the phone with the receiver. She
            composes herself, lifts her suitcase and exits to the
            hotel. Robbie pours himself a drink

IGGY   robbie look – y'know / that was out a order that / a
            mean / a said didn't a say / nothin a could do there
            / didn't know she was gonna – sorry

ROBBIE   sorry / an what ya goin t'do now?

IGGY   do now?

ROBBIE   yes – fuckin do now / what are ya goin t'do now?

IGGY   am not – nothin

ROBBIE   want t'know what i think you should do / she's a
            good woman y'see / vera's a good woman / i think
            you should go up stairs to her / she'll be standin
            outside our room – it's locked / you know the room
            a mean / go up stairs give her those keys an tell her
            yer sorry / i think that would be the thing t'do

IGGY   maybe later robbie – not now / now's not right

ROBBIE   get out t'fuck

IGGY   that wasn't my fault

ROBBIE   get out t'fuck

IGGY   robbie / just let me sit here / a just want t'sit here /
            alright alright look – this is it – this is it / her an
            the kids have left me / everythin's fucked up at the
            moment / a need a bit a time y'know / goin t'get
            her back like / get her back all right / house is
            empty robbie – no one there / just let me sit here

ROBBIE   yer either goin t'walk through that door or i'm goin
            t'throw you out it / what ya want

IGGY   robbie please

ROBBIE   don't have me say it again

            *Iggy finishes his drink and exits to street. Robbie
            sits down beside Joe. He sets the hotel keys on the
            counter.*

JOE   think it's d this time alec

ALEC   it's d – it is d joe

ROBBIE   c it is

            *Vera enters from the hotel. Her and Robbie
            exchange looks. Vera lifts the keys from the counter
            and exits to hotel.*

ALEC   a – it's a joe / a was goin t'say a

ROBBIE   why didn't ya then

ALEC   don't know robbie – just didn't

*End of the day. Slow, very slow. Robbie, Vera, Joe and Alec are
all sitting apart from each other. They all have a drink in front
of them. Varying degrees of drunkenness.*

JOE   what is that we're watchin alec / what is it?

ALEC   that's the news joe

JOE   news aye / alotta people shoutin there alec / looks
           like the lost somethin

ALEC   a lot a people shoutin joe aye

JOE   lost money the have / do all the shoutin in the
           world – not goin t'get it back for them is it / what
           ya think alec not get it back

ALEC   not get it back joe

JOE   what ya reckon robbie / all the shoutin you want
           not get somethin back ya lost

ROBBIE   enough t'loose the have / no damage done

JOE   there speaks a man who knows what he's talkin
           about / a businessman / you know what yer talkin
           about robbie

ROBBIE   aye

JOE   i'd say yer right / the wouldn't have a fuckin clue
           what it's like t'loose somethin / vera

VERA   what?

JOE   they wouldn't have a fuckin clue

VERA   no

JOE   money / aye / different business all t'gether loosin
           yer cat alec – that be a different business

ALEC   a didn't loose the cat joe / don't be sayin a lost the
           cat – a didn't do that

JOE   no alec no / lost as in gone for good / lost as in
           gone forever / never t'return / understan what am
           sayin there alec?

ALEC   not comin back joe

JOE   aye / not fuckin comin back / ya want another
           drink alec / this is the time a day t'rip in t'it / rip in
           t'it now robbie wha / get alec another drink there

ALEC   no more joe

JOE	no more joe
ALEC	time for my bed / listen t'my radio / up early joe – always up early – get the work done
ROBBIE	goin t'have t'go down an sort it out yerself alec
ALEC	the don't like me down there robbie
ROBBIE	it'll be alright alec / just try an keep yer act t'gether
ALEC	am not goin down robbie
ROBBIE	a don't give a fuck alec am tired / am fuckin tired – right
JOE	ya can stay over in my place alec
ROBBIE	what ya mean stay over there?
JOE	what a just said – he can stay over there / that suit ya alec does it
ALEC	suits me fine joe / finish my drink / a need the keys joe
JOE	*throws the keys to Alec* / there ya go
ROBBIE	give 'im the keys back alec / yer not stayin there – he's not stayin there
JOE	fuckin me who says comes an goes / keep the keys alec / away ya go
ROBBIE	he's been drinkin all day / if he goes over there he'll fuckin . . .
JOE	that's where he's goin – over there
ALEC	over there joe
JOE	yer right alec
ALEC	*finishes his drink* / listen t'the radio / up early in the mornin joe
JOE	put all the lights on alec – see where yer at
ALEC	all the lights on joe / *lifts his suitcase* / right robbie / bill day t'morrow vera / get the bill a lizzy t'morrow / right joe

JOE   right alec

            Alec exits to street.

ROBBIE   what the fuck you doin t'me?

JOE   do t'you / fuck all t'do with you

ROBBIE   we talked t'day / i told ya what the fuckin score
            was / we talked t'day / think about it that's what
            you said – you were goin t'fuckin think about it

JOE   thought about fuck all else

ROBBIE   he's goin t'burn the place t'the groun

JOE   that's right – burn the place t'the fuckin groun

ROBBIE   that's right / that's fuckin right / what are ya talkin
            about / i need that place

JOE   the cat's gone robbie / burn the place t'the fuckin
            groun

ROBBIE   no – no no no / the cat's gone / look joe – joe / yer
            head's not right – all the gargle an that / yer sayin
            things there it's all fuckin nonsense / vera tell 'im
            that's all nonsense / joe ya can't burn a house down
            because a fuckin cat left / vera say t'im

VERA   burn it t'the groun joe yer right

JOE   big fire vera

ROBBIE   don't listen t'that joe – she's fuckin / (*to vera*) /
            we're not doin that at the moment right / this is
            somethin else

VERA   burn the place t'the fuckin groun joe

ROBBIE   go crawl after lover boy

VERA   matches / whoof

ROBBIE   it'll be alright joe everythin's soun / yer head's not
            straight at the moment / we'll get alec back / it'll
            be alright

JOE   she's not comin back – ya not understan you stupid
            fuck / she's not comin back

ROBBIE   stop talkin like that / it's a fuckin cat that's all it is
a fuckin cat

JOE   ruby / ruby's not comin back

VERA   hear that robbie / hear what the man's sayin about
his wife

ROBBIE   shut up / i'll go over an get alec / he can stay here /
no harm done if he's here

VERA   not comin back robbie

ROBBIE   what the fuck are you doin?

JOE   *standing over Robbie* / doin / what am a fuckin
doin / burn the place t'the fuckin groun / that's
what am doin

ROBBIE   that it?

JOE   yes / that's it

ROBBIE   been waitin all this time? / sittin there waitin / the
right moment – just pick the right moment

JOE   no / bigger than that / has t'be done / right thing
t'do / can't go home / has t'be fuckin done /
somethin has t'be done / *exiting*

VERA   over t'watch the flames joe

JOE   no

VERA   where you goin then?

JOE   don't know

ROBBIE   that door's getting shut / am closin up

JOE   doesn't matter / not comin back

Joe exits to the street.

VERA   i'm not stayin here robbie

ROBBIE   no

VERA   am tired – am goin t'bed / days are too long in this
place

ROBBIE   aye

VERA   you goin t'lock up?

ROBBIE   i'll lock up / will a leave the front door open for
           'im?

VERA   no / *gives Robbie the hotel keys* / come up t'bed

           Vera exits to hotel. Robbie finishes his drink. He
           walks behind the bar and pours himself a drink.
           Before sitting at the counter he closes the shutters.
           He watches the television.

ROBBIE   fuck

           Robbie switches the television off. He lifts his drink
           then sets it down without taking any. He walks to
           the front door and locks it. He walks back to the
           bar and downs his drink. He turns the lights off
           and exits to the hotel, locking the door behind him.